March of America Facsimile Series

Number 16

Discoverie of the
North Part of Virginia

John Brereton

Discoverie of the North Part of Virginia

by John Brereton

ANN ARBOR

UNIVERSITY MICROFILMS, INC.

A Subsidiary of Xerox Corporation

Foreword

A Briefe and true Relation of the Discoverie of the North part of Virginia...by M. John Brereton, printed in London in 1602, is the first English description of New England and reports the first attempt at its settlement. The author, John Brereton, or Brierton, was a Cambridge-educated minister, who may have met Bartholomew Gosnold through the latter's cousins, residents of a village neighboring that of Brereton's first curacy, Lawshall, Suffolk. This volume reproduces the second impression of the *Relation*, in which a treatise by Captain Edward Hayes and supplementary memoranda by Richard Hakluyt the elder were added.

In this voyage Captain Gosnold's ship, the *Concord*, took a more direct course than ships normally did, which shortened the distance by 1,000 leagues. Off a "mightie headland" that Gosnold named Cape Cod, they found a variety of fish, comparable in numbers to the plenty at Newfoundland, Brereton reported. He wrote enthusiastically of the abundance of fruits, animals, and wildfowl, the richness of the soil, and the plentiful growth of cedar and other trees and valuable sassafras. Brereton found the local Indians gentle and courteous and the climate equally tractable, agreeing so well with English constitutions that "not one of our company...felt the least...inclination to any disease or sicknesse, but were much fatter and in better health than when we went out of England," he boasted. The face of New England could be deceptively fair in the spring, as the Pilgrims were later to discover.

Gosnold had intended to leave a party at a fort constructed on Cuttyhunk Island, but supplies were scanty and few of the ship's company were willing to stay and risk starving. Accordingly, having loaded the ship with furs, cedar logs, and 2,200 lbs. of sassafras, a highly prized diaphoretic, they abandoned the fort and sailed for home on June 18.

There is evidence that Sir Walter Raleigh knew nothing of the expedition until the *Concord* returned to England, despite the dedication to him and the title's claim that he had given permission for the voyage. A satisfactory division of the profits may have placated Raleigh for the infringement of his patent, and he would have recognized the propagandistic value of the tract.

Gosnold's expedition proved the efficacy of the direct course to North America and enlarged English knowledge of the New England coast; and Brereton's account of the valuable commodities of New England and its suitability for settlement stimulated further interest in that area. The voyage of Martin Pring the following year was directly inspired by Brereton's *Relation*. A detailed study of the 1602 expedition will be found in *Bartholomew Gosnold, Discoverer and Planter*, by Warner F. Gookin, completed after Gookin's death by Philip L. Barbour (Hamden, Conn., and London, 1963).

Discoverie of the
North Part of Virginia

A

Briefe and true Relation of
the Discouerie of the North
part of *Virginia*; being a
most pleasant, fruitfull
and commodious
soile:

Made this present yeere 1602, by
Captaine *Bartholomew Gosnold*, Captaine *Bartholowmew Gilbert*, and diuers
other gentlemen their associats, by the
permission of the honourable knight,
Sir WALTER RALEGH, &c.

Written by M. Iohn Brereton
one of the voyage.

Whereunto is annexed a Treatise,
of M. *Edward Hayes*, conteining important
inducements for the planting in those
parts, and finding a passage that
way to the South sea,
and *China*.

*With diuers instructions of speciall moment
newly added in this second impression.*

LONDINI,
Impensis Geor. Bishop.
1602.

To the honourable, Sir WALTER
RALEGH, *Knight*, *Captaine of her*
Maiesties Guards, Lord Warden of the
Stanneries, Lieutenant of *Cornwall*, and
Gouernour of the Ile
of *Iersey*.

 Onourable sir, being earnestly reque∫-
sted by a dœre friend, to put downe in
writing, some true relation of our late
performed voyage to the North parts
of Virginia; at length I resolued to sa-
tisfie his request, who also emboldened
me to direct the same to your honourable consideration; to whom indœd
of duetie it perteineth.

May it please your Lordship therefore to vnderstand, that
vpon the sire and twentieth of March 1602, being Friday,
we went from Falmouth, being in all, two & thirtie persons,
in a small barke of Dartmouth, called The Concord, holding
a course for the North part of Virginia : and although by
chance the winde fauoured vs not at first as we wished, but
inforced vs so farre to the Southward, as we fell with S. Marie, one of the islands of the Açores (which was not much
out of our way) but holding our course directly from thence,
we made our iourney shorter (than hitherto accustomed) by
the better part of a thousand leagues, yet were wœ longer
in our passage than we expected ; which happened, for that
our barke being weake, we were loth to presse her with much
saile ; also, our sailers being few, and they none of the best, we
bare (except in faire weather) but low saile ; besides, our going vpon an vnknowen coast, made vs not ouer-bolde to

They fell with
S. Marie, one of
the Açores.

A 2 stand

land in with the fhoze, but in open weather; which caufed
vs to be certeine daies in founding, befoze we difcouered the
coaft, the weather being by chance, fomewhat foggie. But

They difcoue-
red land the
14.of May.

on Friday the fourteenth of May, early in the mozning, wee
made the land, being full of faire trees, the land fomewhat
low, certeine hummocks oz hilles lying into the land, the
fhoze full of white fand,but very ftony oz rocky.And ftanding
faire alongft by the fhoze, about twelue of the clocke the fame

Eight Indi
ans come a-
boozd of them.

day,we came to an anker, where eight Indians, in a Baske-
fhallop with maft and faile, an iron grapple, and a kettle of
Copper, came boldly aboozd vs,one of them apparelled with a
waftcoat and bzeeches of blacke ferdge, made after our fea-fa-
fhion, hofe and fhoes on his feet; all the reft (fauing one that

The defcrip-
tion of them.

had a paire of bzeeches of blue cloth) were naked. Thefe
people are of tall ftature, bzoad and grim vifage, of a blacke
fwart complexion, their eie-bzowes painted white; their
weapons are bowes and arrowes. It feemed by fome wozds
and fignes they made, that fome Basks oz of S, Iohn de Luz,
haue fifhed oz traded in this place, being in the latitude of 43.
degrees. But riding heere,in no very good harbour, and withall, doubting the weather, about thzee of the clocke the fame
day in the afternoone we weighed, & ftanding Southerly off
into fea the reft of that day and the night following, with a
frefh gale of winde, in the mozning we found our felues em-
baied with a mightie headland; but comming to an anker a-
bout nine of the clocke the fame day, within a league of the

Their firft
landing.

fhoze, we hoifed out the one halfe of our fhallop, and captaine
Bartholmew Gofnold, my felfe, and thzee others,went afhoze,
being a white fandie and very bolde fhoze; and marching all
that afternoone with our muskets on our necks, on the higheft
hilles which we faw (the weather very hot)at length we perceiued this headland to be parcell of the maine, and fundzie
Iflands lying almoft round about it: fo returning (towards
euening) to our fhallop (for by that time, the other part was
bzought afhoze and fet together)we efpied an Indian, a yong

Another In-
dian.

man, of proper ftature, and of a pleafing countenance; and after fome familiaritie with him, we loft him at the feafide, and
returned to our fhip; where, in fiue oz fixe houres abfence, we

Excellent
fifhing.

had peftered our fhip fo with Cod fifh, that we thzew numbers

bers of them ouer-bozd againe : and surely, I am perswaded that in the moneths of March, Apzil, and May,there is
vpon this coast, better fishing, and in as great plentie, as in
Newfound-land : foz the sculles of Mackerell,herrings,Cod,
and other fish, that we daily saw as we went and came from
the shoze, were woonderfull ; and besides, the places where
we tooke these Cods(and might in a few daies haue laden our
ship) were but in seuen fadome water, and within lesse than
a league of the shoze : where, in Newfound-land they fish in
foztie oz fiftie fadome water, and farre off. From this place, A great head-land.
we sailed round about this headland, almost all the points of
the compasse,the shoze very bolde : but as no coast is free from
dangers, so I am persuaded, this is as free as any. The land
somwhat lowe,full of goodly woods,but in some places plaine.
At length we were come amongst many faire Islands, which Many faire Islands.
we had partly discerned at our first landing ; all lying within
a league oz two one of another, and the outermost not aboue
fire oz seuen leagues from the maine : but comming to an anker The first Island called Marthaes vine-yard.
vnder one of them, which was about thzee oz foure leagues
from the maine,captaine Gosnold, my selfe, and some others,
went ashoze,and going round about it, we found it to be foure
English miles in compasse, without house oz inhabitant, sauing a little old house made of boughes, couered with barke,
an olde piece of a weare of the Indians, to catch fish, and one
oz two places, where they had made fires. The chiefest trees
of this Island, are Beeches and Cedars ; the outward parts Beeches. Cedars.
all ouergrowen with lowe bushie trees, thzee oz foure foot in
height, which beare some kinde of fruits, as appeared by
their blossomes ; Strawberries, red and white, as sweet and
much bigger than ours in England : Rasberies, Goseberies,
Hurtleberies, and such an incredible stoze of Wines, aswell Vines in a-bundance.
in the woodie part of the Island, where they run vpon euery
trée, as on the outward parts, that we could not goe foz trea-
ding vpon them : also,many spzings of excellent sweet water, Spzings. A Lake.
and a great standing lake of fresh water, néere the sea side, an
English mile in compasse, which is mainteined with the
spzings running excéeding pleasantly thozow the woodie
grounds which are very rockie. Here are also in this Island,
great stoze of Déere, which we saw, and other beasts, as ap- Deere. Other beasts.

A 3 peared

Cranes.
Hernshawes.
Bitters.
Geese.
Mallards.
Teales.

peared by their tracks; as also diuers fowles, as Cranes, Hernshawes, Bitters, Geese, Mallards, Teales, and other fowles, in great plenty; also, great store of Pease, which grow in certeine plots all the Island ouer. On the North side of this Island we found many huge bones and ribbes of Whales. This Island, as also all the rest of these Islands, are full of all sorts of stones fit for building; the sea sides all couered with stones, many of them glistring and shining like minerall stones, and verie rockie: also, the rest of these Islands are replenished with these commodities, and vpon some of them, inhabitants; as vpon an Island to the Northward, and within two leagues of this; yet wee found no townes, nor many of their houses, although we saw manie Indians, which are tall big boned men, all naked, sauing they couer their priuy parts with a blacke tewed skin, much like a Black smiths apron, tied about their middle and betweene their legs behinde: they gaue vs of their fish readie boiled, (which they carried in a basket made of twigges, not vnlike our osier) whereof we did eat, and iudged them to be fresh water fish: they gaue vs also of their Tabacco, which they drinke greene, but dried into powder, very strong and pleasant, and much better than any I haue tasted in England: the necks of their pipes are made of clay hard dried, (whereof in that Island is great store both red and white) the other part is a piece of hollow copper, very finely closed and semented together. Wee gaue vnto them certeine trifles, as kniues, points, and such like, which they much esteemed. From hence we went to another Island, to the Northwest of this, and within a league or two of the maine, which we found to bee greater than before we imagined, being 16. English miles at the least in compasse; for it conteineth many pieces or necks of land, which differ nothing from seuerall Islands, sauing that certeine banks of small bredth, do like bridges, ioine them to this Island. On the outsides of this Island are many plaine places of grasse, abundance of Strawberies & other berries before mentioned. In mid May we did sowe in this Island (for a triall) in sundry places, Wheat, Barley, Oats, and Pease, which in fourteene daies were sprung vp nine inches and more. The soile is fat and lustie, the vpper crust of gray colour,

colour; but a foot oꝛ leſſe in depth, of the colour of our hempe-
lands in England; and being thus apt foꝛ theſe and the like
graines; the ſowing oꝛ ſetting (after the ground is clenſed)
is no greater labour, than if you ſhould ſet oꝛ ſow in one of
our beſt pꝛepared gardens in England. This Iſland is full of
high timbꝛed Dakes, their leaues thꝛiſe ſo bꝛoad as ours; Ce-
ders, ſtraight and tall; Béech, Elme, hollie, Walnut trées in a-
boundance, the fruit as bigge as ours, as appeared by thoſe
we found vnder the trées, which had lien all the yére vnga-
thered; Haſlenut trées, Cherry trées, the leafe, barke and bigneſſe not differing from ours in England, but the ſtalke beareth the bloſſoms oꝛ fruit at the end thereof, like a cluſter of
Grapes, foꝛty oꝛ fifty in a bunch; Saſſafras trées great plentie all the Iſland ouer, a trée of high pꝛice and pꝛofit; alſo diuers other fruit trées, ſome of them with ſtrange barkes, of an
Oꝛange colour, in féeling ſoft and ſmothe like Veluet: in the
thickeſt parts of theſe woods, you may ſée a furlong oꝛ moꝛe
round about. On the Noꝛthweſt ſide of this Iſland, nére to
the ſea ſide, is a ſtanding Lake of freſh water, almoſt thꝛée
Engliſh miles in compaſſe, in the middeſt whereof ſtands a
plot of woody ground, an acre in quantitie oꝛ not aboue:
this Lake is full of ſmall Toꝛtoiſes, and exceedingly frequented with all ſoꝛts of fowles befoꝛe rehearſed, which bꝛæd,
ſome low on the banks, and others on low trées about this
Lake in great aboundance, whoſe yong ones of all ſoꝛts we
toke and eat at our pleaſure: but all theſe fowles are much
bigger than ours in England. Alſo, in euery Iſland, and almoſt in euery part of euery Iſland, are great ſtoꝛe of Ground
nuts, foꝛtie together on a ſtring, ſome of them as bigge as
hennes egges; they grow not two inches vnder ground: the
which nuts we found to be as good as Potatoes. Alſo, diuers
ſoꝛts of ſhell-fiſh, as Scalops, Muſcles, Cockles, Lobſters,
Crabs, Oiſters, and Wilks, exceeding good and very great.
But not to cloy you with particular rehearſall of ſuch things
as God & Nature hath beſtowed on theſe places, in compari-
ſon whereof, the moſt fertil part of al England is (of it ſelfe) but
barren; we went in our light-hoꝛſman from this Iſland to the
maine, right againſt this Iſland ſome two leagues off, where
comming aſhoꝛe, we ſtod a while like men rauiſhed at the

A 4　　　　　　　　　　　beautie

Dakes.
Cedars.
Beech.
Elme.
Hollie.
Walnut trees.
Cherry trees.

Saſſafras
trees.
Diuers other
trees.

A lake thꝛée
miles about.

Small Toꝛ-
toiſes.

Abundance of
fowles, much
bigger than
ours in Eng-
land.
Ground nuts.

Shell fiſh.

The exceeding beautie of the maine land. Great Lakes. Large medowes

beautie and delicacie of this sweet soile ; for besides diuers cleere Lakes of fresh water (whereof we saw no end) Medowes very large and full of grǽne grasse ; euen the most woody places (I speake onely of such as I saw) doe grow so distinct and apart, one trǽ from another, vpon grǽne grassie ground, somewhat higher than the Plaines, as if Nature would shew her selfe aboue her power, artificiall. Hard by, we espied seuen Indians, and cumming vp to them, at first

Seuen Indians.

they expressed some feare ; but being emboldned by our curteous vsage, and some trifles which we gaue them, they followed vs to a necke of land, which we imagined had bǽne seuered from the maine ; but finding it otherwise, we perceiued

A broad riuer.

a broad harbour or riuers mouth, which ranne vp into the maine : and because the day was farre spent, we were forced to returne to the Island from whence we came, leauing the

A good harbour.

discouery of this harbour, for a time of better leasure. Of the goodnesse of which harbour, as also of many others thereabouts, there is small doubt, considering that all the Islands, as also the maine (where we were) is all rockie grounds and broken lands. Now the next day, we determined to fortifie our selues in a little plot of ground in the midst of the Lake

The English house.

aboue mentioned, where we built an house, and couered it with sedge, which grew about this lake in great aboundance ; in building whereof, we spent thrǽ wǽks and more : but the second day after our comming from the maine, we espied 11

Eleuen canowes with fiftie Indians in them.

canowes or boats, with fiftie Indians in them, comming toward vs from this part of the maine, where we, two daies before landed ; and being loth they should discouer our fortification, we went out on the sea side to mǽte them ; and comming somewhat nǽre them, they all sat downe vpon the stones, calling aloud to vs (as we rightly ghessed) to doe the like, a little distance from them : hauing sat a while in this order, captaine Gosnold willed me to goe vnto them, to sǽ what countenance they would make ; but as soone as I came vp vnto them, one of them, to whom I had giuen a knife two daies before in the maine, knew me, (whom I also very wel remembred) and smiling vpon me, spake somewhat vnto their lord

Their captaine.

or captaine, which sat in the midst of them, who presently rose vp and tooke a large Beauer skin from one that stood about him

him, and gaue it vnto me, which I requited for that time the best I could : but I, pointing towards captaine Gosnold, made signes vnto him, that he was our captaine, and desirous to be his friend, and enter league with him, which (as I perceiued) he vnderstood, and made signes of ioy : whereupon captaine Gosnold with the rest of his companie, being twenty in all, came vp vnto them ; and after many sigues of gratulations (captaine Gosnold presenting their Lord with certaine trifles which they wondred at, and highly esteemed) we became very great friends, and sent for meat abord our shallop, and gaue them such meats as we had then readie dressed ; whereof they misliked nothing but our mustard, whereat they made many a sowre face. While we were thus mery, one of them had conueied a target of ours into one of their canowes, which we suffered, onely to trie whether they were in subiection to this Lord to whom we made signes (by shewing him another of the same likenesse, and pointing to the canow) what one of his companie had done : who suddenly expressed some feare, and speaking angerly to one about him (as we perceiued by his countenance) caused it presently to be brought backe againe. So the rest of the day we spent in trading with them for Furres, which are Beauers, Luzernes, Marterns, Otters, Wild-cat skinnes, very large and deepe Furre, blacke Foxes, Conie skinnes, of the colour of our Hares, but somewhat lesse, Deare skinnes, very large, Seale skinnes, and other beasts skinnes, to vs vnknowen. They haue also great store of Copper, some very redde, and some of a paler colour ; none of them but haue chaines, earings or collars of this mettall : they head some of their arrows herewith much like our broad arrow heads, very workmanly made. Their chaines are many hollow pieces semented together, ech piece of the bignesse of one of our reeds, a finger in length, ten or twelue of them together on a string, which they weare about their necks : their collars they weare about their bodies like bandelieres a handfull broad, all hollow pieces, like the other, but somewhat shorter, four hundred pieces in a collar, very fine and euenly set together. Besides these, they haue large drinking cups made like sculles, and other thinne plates of copper, made

B   much

Seuerall sorts of Furres.

Red Copper in abundance.

Chaines.

Collars.

Drinking cuppes of Copper.

much like our boare-speare blades, all which they so little esteeme, as they offered their fairest collars or chaines, for a knife or such like trifle, but we seemed little to regard it; yet I was desirous to vnderstand where they had such store of this mettall, and made signes to one of them (with whom I was very familiar) who taking a piece of Copper in his hand, made a hole with his finger in the ground, and withall pointed to the maine from whence they came. They strike fire in this manner; euery one carrieth about him in a purse of tewd leather, a Minerall stone (which I take to be their Copper) and with a flat Emerie stone (wherewith Glasiers cut glasse, and Cutlers glase blades) tied fast to the end of a little sticke, gently he striketh vpon the Minerall stone, and within a stroke or two, a sparke falleth vpon a piece of Touchwood (much like our Spunge in England) and with the least sparke he maketh a fire presently. We had also of their Flaxe, wherewith they make many strings and cords, but it is not so bright of colour as ours in England: I am perswaded they haue great store growing vpon the maine, as also Mines and many other rich commodities, which we, wanting both time and meanes, could not possibly discouer. Thus they continued with vs three daies, euery night retiring themselues to the furthermost part of our Island two or three miles from our fort: but the fourth day they returned to the maine, pointing fiue or six times to the Sun, and once to the maine, which we vnderstood, that within fiue or six daies they would come from the maine to vs againe: but being in their canowes a little from the shore, they made huge cries & shouts of ioy vnto vs; and we with our trumpet and cornet, and casting vp our cappes into the aire, made them the best farewell we could: yet six or seuen of them remained with vs behinde, bearing vs company euery day into the woods, and helpt vs to cut and carie our Sassafras, and some of them lay aboord our ship. These people, as they are exceeding courteous, gentle of disposition, and well conditioned, excelling all others that we haue seene; so for shape of bodie and louely fauour, I thinke they excell all the people of America; of stature much higher than we; of complexion or colour, much like a darke Oliue; their eie-browes and haire blacke, which they weare

Mines of Copper.

Minerall stones.

Emerie stones.

Flaxe.

Indians apt for seruice.

Sassafras.

A goodly people, & of good conditions.

weare long, tied vp behinde in knots, whereon they pricke
feathers of fowles, in fashion of a crownet: some of them are
blacke thin bearded; they make beards of the haire of beasts:
and one of them offered a beard of their making to one of our
sailers, for his that grew on his face, which because it was of
a red colour, they iudged to be none of his owne. They are
quicke eied, and stedfast in their looks, fearelesse of others
harmes, as intending none themselues; some of the meaner
sort giuen to filching, which the very name of Saluages (not
weighing their ignorance in good or euill) may easily excuse:
their garments are of Deere skins, and some of them weare   *Their appa-*
Furres round and close about their necks. They pronounce   *rell.*
our language with great facilitie; for one of them one day
sitting by mee, vpon occasion I spake smiling to him these
words: How now (sirrha) are you so saucie with my Tabacco?
which words (without any further repetition) he suddenly
spake so plaine and distinctly, as if he had béene a long scholar
in the language. Many other such trials we had, which are
héere néedlesse to repeat. Their women (such as we saw)   *Their wo-*
which were but thrée in all, were but lowe of stature, their   *men.*
eie-browes, haire, apparell, and maner of wearing, like to
the men, fat, and very well fauoured, and much delighted in
our company; the men are very dutifull towards them. And
truely, the holsomnesse and temperature of this Climat, doth
not onely argue this people to be answerable to this description, but also of a perfect constitution of body, actiue, strong,
healthfull, and very wittie, as the sundry toies of theirs cun-   *The goodnesse*
ningly wrought, may easily witnes. For the agréeing of this   *of the Climat.*
Climat with vs (I speake of my selfe, & so I may iustly do for
the rest of our company) that we found our health & strength
all the while we remained there, so to renew and increase,
as notwithstanding our diet and lodging was none of the
best, yet not one of our company (God be thanked) felt the
least grudging or inclination to any disease or sicknesse, but
were much fatter and in better health than when we went
out of England. But after our barke had taken in so much
Sassafras, Cedar, Furres, Skinnes, and other commodities,
as were thought conuenient; some of our company that had
promised captaine Gosnold to stay, hauing nothing but a sa-

 uing voyage in their minds, made our company of inhabitants (which was small enough before) much smaller; so as captaine Gosnold seeing his whole strength to consist but of twelue men, and they but meanly prouided, determined to **Their retnrn.** returne for England, leauing this Island (which he called Elizabeths Island) with as many true sorrowfull eies, as were before desirous to see it. So the 18. of June, being Friday, we weighed, and with indifferent faire winde and weather came to anker the 23 of July, being also Friday (in all, bare fiue weeks) before Exmouth.

Your Lordships to command,
Ihon Brereton.

A briefe Note of such commodities as we saw
in the countrey, notwithstanding our small time of stay.

Trees.

SAssafras trees, the roots wherof at 3. s. the pound are 336. l. the tunne.
Cedars tall and straight, in great abundance.
Cypres trees.
Oakes.
Walnut trees great store.
Elmes.
Beech.
Hollie.
Haslenut trees.
Cherry trees.
Cotten trees.
Other fruit trees to vs vnknowen.

The finder of our Sassafras in these parts, was one Master Robert Meriton.

Fowles.

EAgles.
Hernshawes.
Cranes.
Bitters.
Mallards.
Teales.
Geese.
Pengwins.
Ospreis and Hawks.
Crowes.
Rauens.
Mewes.
Doues.
Sea-pies.
Blacke-birds with carnation wings.

Beasts.

DEere in great store, very great and large.
Beares.

Beares.
Luzernes.
Blacke Foxes.
Beauers.
Otters.
Wilde-Cats, verie large and
  great.
Dogs like Foxes, blacke and
  sharpe nosed.
Conies.

Fruits, Plants, and Herbs.

TAbacco, excellent sweet
  and strong.
Vines in more plenty than in
  France.
Ground-nuts, good meat, &
  also medicinable.
Strawberries.
Raspeberries.
Gooseberries.
Hurtleberries.
Pease growing naturally.
Flaxe.

Iris Florentina, whereof apo-
  thecaries make sweet balles.
Sorrell, and many other herbs
  wherewith they made sal-
  lets.

Fishes.

WHales.
  Tortoises, both on
  land and sea.
Seales.
Cods.
Mackerell.
Breames.
Herrings.
Thornbacke.
Hakes.
Rockefish.
Doggefish.
Lobstars.
Crabbes.
Muscles.
Wilks.
Cockles.
Scallops.
Oisters.

SNakes foure foot in length, and sixe inches about, which
  the Indians eat for daintie meat, the skinnes whereof they
  vse for girdles.
Colours to die with, red, white, and blacke.

Mettals and Stones.

COpper in great abun-
  dance.
Emerie stones for Glasiers &
  Cutlers.
Alabaster very white.
Stones glistering and shining
  like Minerall stones.

Stones of a blue mettalline
  colour, which we take to be
  Steele oare.
Stones of all sorts for buildings.
Clay, red & white, which may
  proue good Terra Sigillata.

B 3   A briefe

A briefe Note of the sending another barke
this present yeere 1602. *by the honorable*
knight, Sir WALTE RALEGH,
for the searching out of his
Colonie in *Virginia.*

 Amuel Mace of Weimouth, a very sufficent Mariner, an honest sober man, who had bæne at Virginia twise befoze, was imploied thither by Sir Walter Ralegh, to finde those people which were left there in the yære 1587. To whose succour he hath sent fiue seuerall times at his owne charges. The parties by him set fozth, perfozmed nothing; some of them following their owne pzofit elsewhere; others returning with friuolous allegations. At this last time, to auoid all excuse, he bought a barke, and hired all the company foz wages by the moneth: who departing from Weimouth in March last 1602, fell foztie leagues to the Southwestward of Hatarask, in thirtie foure degrées oz thereabout; and hauing there spent a moneth; when they came along the coast to sæke the people, they did it not, pzetending that the extremitie of weather and losse of some pzincipall ground-tackle, fozced and feared them from searching the pozt of Hatarask, to which they were sent. From that place where they abode, they bzought Sassafras, Radix Chinæ oz the China rœt, Beniamin, Cassia, lignea, & a rinde of a trée moze strong than any spice as yet knowen, with diuers other commodities, which hereafter in a larger discourse may come to light.
* *
*

A Treatise

A Treatife, conteining important induce-
ments *for the planting in thefe parts*, *and*
finding a paffage that way to the
South fea and China.

He voiage which we intend, is to plant Chri- **Temperate Climats.**
ftian people and religion vpon the Northweft
countries of America, in places temperat and
well agræing with our conftitution, which
though the fame doe lie betwæne 40. and 44.
degræs of latitude, vnder the Paralels of Italy
and France, yet are not they fo hot; by reafon that the funs heat
is qualified in his courfe ouer the Ocean, befoze he arriueth
vpon the coafts of America, attracting much vapour from the
fea: which mitigation of his heat, we take foz a benefit to vs
that intend to inhabit there; becaufe vnder the Climat of 40
degræs, the fame would be too vehement els foz our bodies to
endure.

These lands were neuer yet actually poffeffed by any Chri- **Her Maiefties title.**
ftian pzince oz people, yet often intended to be by the French
nation, which long fithence had inhabited there, if domefticall
warres had not withheld them: notwithftanding the fame
are the rightfull inheritance of her Maieftie, being firft difcouered by our nation in the time of King Henrie the feuenth,
vnder the conduct of Iohn Cabot and his fonnes: by which
title of firft difcouery, the kings of Portugall and Spaine doe
holde and enioy their ample and rich kingdomes in their Indies Eaft and Weft; and alfo lately planted in part by the
Colonies fent thither by the honourable knight, Sir Walter
Ralegh.

The courfe vnto thefe countreys, is thozow the Ocean, al- **A commodi-ous and fafe courfe.**
together frée from all reftraint by fozren pzinces to be made;
whereunto other our accuftomed trades are fubiect; apt foz
moft winds that can blow, to be perfozmed commonly in 30

o2 35 daies. The coaſt faire, with ſafe roads and harbo2s fo2 ſhips: Many riuers.

Riuers.

Fertile lands.

Theſe lands be faire and pleaſant, reſembling France, intermedled with mountaines, valleys, medowes, woodlands, and champians. The ſoile is excæding ſtrong, by reaſon it was neuer manured ; and will be therefo2e moſt fit to beare at firſt, Rape-ſæds, Hempe, Flax, and whatſoeuer els requireth ſuch ſtrong ſoile. Rape-oiles, and all ſo2ts of oiles, will be very commodious fo2 England, which ſpendeth oiles aboundantly about Clothing and Leather-d2eſſing. In like ſo2t, Hempe and Flax are p2ofitable, whether the ſame be ſent into England, o2 w2ought there by our people ; Wad alſo will grow there aſwell o2 better then in Terçera.

Rape oiles.

The Saluages weare faire colours in ſome of their atire, whereby we hope to finde rich dies and colours fo2 painting.

Dies.

The træs are fo2 the moſt part, Cedars, Pines, Sp2uſe, Firre and Oaks to the No2thward. Of theſe træs will be d2awen Tarre and Pitch, Roſen, Turpentine, and Soape-aſhes: They will make maſts fo2 the greateſt ſhippes of the wo2ld: Excellent timbers of Cedar, and bo2ds fo2 curious building.

The cliffes vpon the coaſts and mountaines euery where ſhew great likelihod of Minerals. A very rich mine of Copper is found, whereof I haue ſæne p2oofe ; and the place deſcribed. Not farre from which there is great hope alſo of a Siluer mine. There be faire quarries of ſtone, of beautifull colours, fo2 buildings.

Minerals.
Copper.

The ground b2ingeth fo2th, without induſtrie, Peaſe, Roſes, G2apes, Hempe, beſides other plants, fruits, herbs and flowers, whoſe pleaſant view and delectable ſmelles, doe demonſtrate ſufficiently the fertility and ſwætneſſe of that ſoile and aire.

G2apes.

Beaſts of many kindes ; ſome of the bigneſſe of an D2e, whoſe hides make good buffe: Dære, both red and of other ſo2ts in aboundance: Luzerns, Marterns, Sables, Beauers, Beares, Otters, Wolues, Foxes, and Squirrels, which to the No2thward are blacke, and accounted very rich furres.

Beaſts.

Fowles both of the water and land, infinit ſto2e and varietie ; Hawks both ſho2t and long winged, Partriges in aboundance,

Fowles.

bundance, which are verie great, and easily taken. Birds great and small, some like vnto our Blacke-birds, others like Canarie-birds: And many (as well birds as other creatures) ſtrange and differing from ours of Europe.

Fiſh, namely, Cods, which as we encline moze vnto the South, are moze large and vendible foz England and France, then the Newland fiſh. Whales and Seales in great abundances. Diles of them are rich commodities foz England, whereof we now make Soape, beſides many other vſes. Item, Tunneys, Anchoues, Bonits, Salmons, Lobſters, Diſters hauing Pearle, and infinit other ſozts of fiſh, which are moze plentifull vpon thoſe Nozthweſt coaſts of America, than in any parts of the knowen wozld. Salt is repozted to be found there, which els may be made there, to ſerue ſufficiently foz all fiſhing.

So as the commodities there to be raiſed both of the ſea and land (after that we haue planted our people ſkilfull and induſtrious) will be, Fiſh, Whale and Seale oiles, Soape aſhes and Soape, Tarre and Pitch, Roſen and Turpentine, Maſts, Timber and bozds of Cedars, Firres, and Pines, Hempe, Flaxe, Cables and Ropes, Saile-clothes, Grapes, and Raiſens and Wines, Cozne, Rape-ſæds & oiles, Hides, Skinnes, Furres, Dies and Colours foz painting, Pearle, Mettals, and other Minerals.

Commodities in generall.

Theſe commodities befoze rehearſed, albeit foz the moſt part they be groſſe, yet are the ſame profitable foz the State of England ſpecially, aſwell in regard of the vſe of ſuch commodities, as foz the imploiment alſo of our people and ſhips; the want whereof, doth decay our townes and pozts of England, and cauſeth the realme to ſwarme full with poze and idle people.

Imploiment of our people, and repairing decaied pozts.

Theſe commodities in like ſozt, are of great vſe and eſtimation in all the South and Weſterne countreys of Europe; namely, Italie, France and Spaine; foz the which all nations that haue bæne accuſtomed to repaire vnto the Newfoundland foz the commoditie of fiſh and oiles alone, will hencefozward fozſake the Newfound-land, and trade with vs, when once we haue planted people in thoſe parts: by whoſe induſtrie ſhall be pzouided foz all commers, both fiſh and oiles,

The trade to Newfound-land ſhalbe removed to vs.

C   and

and many commodities befides, of good importance & value.

Spanifh commodities.

Then will the Spaniards and Portugals bring vnto vs in exchange of fuch commodities before mentioned, Wines, Swæt oiles, Fruits, Spices, Sugars, Silks, Gold and Siluer, or whatfoeuer that Europe yældeth, to fupply our neceffities, and to increafe our delights.

Englifh commodities.

For which Spanifh commodities and other forts likewife, our merchants of England will bring vnto vs againe, Cloth, Cattell, for our ftore and bræd, and euery thing els that we fhall næd, or that England fhall haply exchange for fuch commodities.

Uent of our Cloth.

By this intercourfe, our habitations will be made a Staple of all vendible commodities of the world, and a meanes to vent a very great quantitie of our Englifh cloth into all the cold regions of America extended very farre.

Intercourfe will foone be had with other nacions.

This intercourfe alfo will be foone drawen together by this reafon: That nære adioining vpon the fame coafts of Newfound-land, is the greateft fifhing of the world; whether doe yærely repaire about 400 failes of fhips, for no other commoditie than Fifh and Whale-oiles. Then forafmuch as merchants are diligent inquifitours after gaines, they will foone remooue their trade from Newfound-land vnto vs nære at hand, for fo great increafe of gaine as they fhall make by trading with vs. For whereas the voyage vnto the Newfoundland is into a more cold and intemperate place, not to be traded nor frequented at all times, nor fortified for fecuritie of the fhips and goods; oft fpoiled by pirats or men of warre; the charges great for falt; double manning and double victualling their fhips, in regard that the labor is great and the time long, before their lading can be made readie: they cary outwards no commodities for fraight; and after fire moneths voyage, their returne is made but of Fifh and Oiles.

Incommodities in the Newland trade.

Commodities by hauing trade with vs.

Contrariwife, by trading with vs at our intended place, the courfe fhalbe in a maner as fhort; into a more temperate and healthfull climat; at all times of the yære to be traded; harbors fortified to fecure fhips and goods; charges abridged of falt, victualling and manning fhips double: becaufe lading fhall be prouided vnto their hands at a more eafie rate than themfelues could make it. They fhall carry fraight alfo outward

ward, to make exchange with vs; and so get profit both
waies: and then euery foure moneths they may make a voyage and returne, of both fish and oiles, and many other commodities of good worth.

These reasons aduisedly waighed, shall make our enter- *Note.*
prise appeare easie, and the most profitable of the world, for
our nation to vndertake. The reasons we chiefly relie vpon are these, namely.

1. Those lands which we intend to inhabit, shall minister
   vnto our people, the subiect and matter of many notable commodities.
2. England shall afford vs people both men, women and
   children aboue 10000, which may very happily be
   spared from hence to worke those commodities there.
3. Newfound-land shall minister shipping to carrie away
   all our commodities, and to bring others vnto vs a-
   gaine for our supplie.

Now two of these reasons are already effected vnto our An easie en-
hands: that is to say: The place where we shall finde rich terprise, and
commodities, and ships to vent them. It remaineth onely great reward.
for our parts, to carrie and transport people with their pro-
uisions from England, where the miserie and necessitie of ma-
nie crie out for such helpe and reliefe.

This considered, no nation of Christendom is so fit for this The English
action as England, by reason of our superfluous people (as I nation most
may tearme them) and of our long domesticall peace. And fit for disco-
after that we be once 200 men strong, victualled and fortifi- ueries.
ed, we can not be remoued by as many thousands.

For besides that, we haue seene both in France and the
Low-countreys, where 200 men well fortified and victualled,
haue kept out the forces both of the French & Spanish kings,
euen within their owne kingdomes: it shall be also a matter
of great difficulty, to transport an army ouer the Ocean with
victuals and munition, and afterwards to abide long siege a-
broad, against vs fortified within, where the very elements
and famine shall fight for vs, though we should lie still and
defend onely.

C 2   The

The Saluages vnable to defend oz offend.

The Saluages neither in this attempt shall hurt vs, they being simple, naked and vnarmed, destitute of edge-tooles oz weapons; whereby they are vnable either to defend theselues oz to offend vs: neither is it our intent to pzouoke, but to cherrish and win them vnto Chzistianitie by faire meanes; yet not to trust them to far, but to pzouide against all accidents.

Then to conclude, as we of all other nations are most fit foz a discouery and planting in remote places; euen so, vnder the heauens there is no place to be found so conuenient foz such a purpose; by reason of the temperature, commodities, apt site foz trade, & repaire thither already of so many ships, which in any other frequented countrey, can not be pzocured in a mans age, noz with expense of halfe a million.

This action but set on foot, will goe foz ward of it selfe.

So as the onely difficultie now, is in our first pzeparation to transpozt some few people at the beginning; the charges whereof shall be defraied by our first returne, of fish and some commodities of Sassafras, Hides, Skinnes and Furres, which we shall also haue by trading with the Saluages. The pzofe of which commodities shall incourage our merchants to venter largely in the next. The supplie shall easily and continually be sent by ships, which yeerely goe from hence vnto the Newfound-land and vs; and the intercourse & exchange we shall haue with all nations repairing thither, shall stoze vs with aboundance of all things foz our necessities and de-

Ouersight in choise of a new habitation.

lightes. Which reasons if they had beene fozeseene of them that planted in the South part of Virginia (which is a place destitute of good harbours, and farre from all trade) no doubt but if they had settled neerer vnto this frequented trade in the Newfound-land, they had by this time beene a flourishing State, and plentifull in all things; who also might then haue made way into the bowels of that large continent, where assuredly we shall discouer very goodly and rich kingdomes and cities.

A matter of impoztance foz England.

It may also seeme a matter of great consequence foz the good and securitie of England; that out of these Moztherly regions we shall be able to furnish this realme of all maner of pzouisions foz our nauies; namely, Pitch, Rosen, Cables, Ropes, Masts, and such like; which shall be made within those her Maiesties owne dominions, by her owne subiects,

and

and brought hither thorow the Ocean, frō from reſtraint of any other prince ; whereby the cuſtomes and charges beſtowed by our merchants (to the inriching of forren Eſtates) ſhall be leſſened, and turned to the benefit of her Highneſſe and her Deputies in thoſe parts : which alſo ſhall deliuer our merchants from many troubles & moleſtations which they now vnwillingly indure in our Eaſt trades ; and ſhall make vs the leſſe to doubt the malice of thoſe States whom now we may not offend, leſt we ſhould be intercepted of the ſame prouiſions, to the weakening of our nauie, the moſt roiall defence of this noble realme.

Of a conuenient paſſage and trade into the
South Sea, vnder temperate regions, part by riuers, and ſome part ouer land, in the continent of *America*.

I Will adde hereunto an aſſured hope (grounded vpon infallible reaſons) of a way to be made part ouerland, & part by riuers or lakes, into the South ſeas vnto Cathay, China, and thoſe paſſing rich countreys, lying in the Eaſt parts of the world : which way or paſſage (ſuppoſed to be beyond the vttermoſt bounds of America, vnder the frozen Zone) is neuertheleſſe, held by the opinion of many learned writers and men of iudgement now liuing, to be in theſe more temperate rigions ; and that the ſame ſhall neuer be made knowen, vnleſſe we plant firſt ; whereby we ſhall learne as much by inquiſition of the naturall inhabitants, as by our owne nauigations. I will not herein relie vpon reports made in the French mens diſcoueries ; that the ſea which giueth paſſage vnto Cathay, extendeth from the North, nære vnto the riuer of Canada, into 44 degrées, where the ſame of the Saluages is called Tadouac.

Neither vpon the diſcoueries of Iaques Noel, who hauing paſſed beyond the three Saults, where Iaques Cartier left to diſcouer, finding the riuer of S. Laurence paſſable on the other ſide or branch; and afterwards, vnderſtood of the inhabitants, that the ſame riuer did lead into a mighty lake, which at

the

the entrance was frefh , but beyond , was bitter oꝛ falt ; the end whereof was vnknowen.

Omitting therefoꝛe thefe hopes , I will ground my opinion vpon reafon and nature, which will not faile.

Foꝛ this we know alreadie , that great riuers haue béene difcouered a thoufand Englifh miles into that continent of America; namely, that of S. Laurence oꝛ Canada. But not regarding miles moꝛe oꝛ leffe , moft affuredly , that and other knowen riuers there doe defcend from the higheft parts oꝛ mountaines , oꝛ middle of that continent, into our Noꝛth fea.

A large courfe of a riuer thorowa mightie continent, pꝛoduceth a poꝛtable riuer.

And like as thofe mountains doe caft from them, ftreames into our Noꝛth feas; euen fo the like they doe into the South fea, which is on the backe of that continent.

Foꝛ all mountaines haue their defcents toward the feas about them, which are the loweft places and pꝛoper manfions of water : and waters (which are contained in the mountaines , as it were in cifternes) defcending naturally , doe alwaies refoꝛt vnto the feas inuironing thofe lands : foꝛ example ; from the Alps confining Germanie, France, and Italie, the mighty riuer Danubie doth take his courfe Eaft , and difchargeth into the Pontique fea : the Rhine, Noꝛth, and falleth into the Germane fea : the Rhofne , Weft , and goeth into the Mediterran fea : the Po, South, is emptied into the Adriatick oꝛ gulfe of Venice. other inftances may be pꝛoduced to like effect in Africk ; yea, at home amongft the mountaines in England.

Séeing then in nature this can not be denied , and by experience elfewhere is found to be fo , I will fhew how a trade may be difpofed moꝛe commodioufly into the South fea thorow thefe temperate and habitable regions , than by the froꝛen Zones in the fuppofed paffages of Noꝛthweft oꝛ Noꝛtheaft : where, if the very moment be omitted of the time to paffe , then are we like to be froꝛen in the feas, oꝛ foꝛced to Winter in extreame cold and darkeneffe like vnto hell : oꝛ in the midft of Summer , we fhalbe in perill to haue our fhips ouerwhelmed oꝛ crufht in pieces by hideous and fearefull mountaines of yce floting vpon thofe feas.

Therefoꝛe foure Staple-places muft be erected , when the moft fhoꝛt and paffable way is found : that is to fay, two

vpon

vpon the Nozth side, at the head and fall of the riuer ; and two others on the South side, at the head and fall also of that other riuer.

Prouided , that ships may passe vp those riuers vnto the Staples , so farre as the same be nauigable into the land ; and afterwards , that boats with flat bottomes may also passe so high and nære the heads of the riuers vnto the Staples, as possibly they can , euen with lesse than two foot water, which can not then be far from the heads ; as in the riuer of Chagre.

That necke oz space of land betwæne the two heads of the said riuers , if it be 100 leagues (which is not like) the com-modities from the Nozth and from the South sea bzought thither, may wel be carried ouer the same vpon hozses, mules oz beasts of that countrey apt to labour (as the elke oz buffel) oz by the aid of many Saluages accustomed to burdens ; who shall stead vs greatly in these affaires.

It is mozeouer to be considered, that all these countreys do yæld (so farre as is knowen) Cedars, Pines, Firre træs and Daks, to build, mast, and yeard ships ; wherefoze we may not doubt, but that ships may be builded on the South sea.

Then as ships on the South side may goe and returne to and from Cathay , China , and other most rich regions of the East wozld in fiue moneths oz thereabouts ; euen so the goods being carried ouer vnto the Nozth side, ships may come thi-ther from England to fetch the same goods , and returne by a voyage of foure oz fiue moneths vsually.

So as in euery foure moneths may be returned into Eng-land the greatest riches of Cathay, China, Iapan, and the rest which will be Spices , Dzugges , Muske , Pearle, Stones, Gold, Siluer, Silks, Clothes of gold, & all maner of pzecious things , which shall recompense the time and labour of their transpoztation and carriage, if it were as farre and dange-rous as the Moozes trade is from Fess and Marocco (ouez the burning and moueable sands, in which they perish many times , and suffer commonly great distresses) vnto the riuer called Niger in Africa , and from thence, vp the said riuer ma-nie hundzed miles ; afterwards ouer-land againe, vnto the riuer Nilus; and so vnto Cairo in Egypt, from whence they returne the way they came.

Oꝛ if it were a voyage fo farre as our merchants haue made into Perſia, euen to Ormus, by the way of the Noꝛth, thꝛough Ruſsia into the Caſpian ſea, and fo foꝛth, with pai-ment of many tolles. But this paſſage ouer and thoꝛow the continent of America,, as the ſame ſhall be alwaies vnder temperate and habitable climats, and a pleaſant paſſage af-ter it hath béene a little frequented: euen fo it muſt fall out much ſhoꝛter than it ſæmeth, by falſe deſcription of that con-tinent, which doth not extend fo farre into the Weſt, as by later nauigations is found and deſcribed in moꝛe ex-quiſit charts. Beſides that, the ſea extends it ſelfe into the land very farre in many places on the South ſide; whereby our acceſſe vnto the South ocean, ſhall be by fo much the ſhoꝛter.

FINIS.

Inducements to the liking of the voyage intended *towards* Virginia *in* 40. *and* 42. *degrees*
of latitude, written 1 5 8 5. by M. *Richard*
Hakluyt the elder, sometime student of
the Middle Temple.

He glozy of God by planting of religion a-
mong those infidels.

2 The increase of the force of the Christians.

3 The possibilitie of the inlarging of the dominions of the Quéenes most excellent Ma-
iestie, and consequently of her honour, reue-
nues, and of her power by this enterpzise.

4 An ample vent in time to come of the Woollen clothes
of England, especially those of the coursest sozts, to the maintenance of our pooze, that els sterue oz become burdensome to
the realme: and vent also of sundzy our commodities vpon the
tract of that firme land, and possibly in other regions from the
Noztherne side of that maine.

5 A great possibilitie of further discoueries of other regions from the Nozth part of the same land by sea, and of vn-
speakable honoz and benefit that may rise vpon the same, by
the trades to ensue in Iapan, China, and Cathay, &c.

6 By returne thence, this realme shall receiue (by reason
of the situation of the climate, and by reason of the excellent
soile) Dade, Oile, Wines, Hops, Salt, and most oz all the commodities that we receiue from the best parts of Europe, and
we shall receiue the same better cheape, than now we receiue
them, as we may vse the matter.

7 Receiuing the same thence, the nauie, the humane
strength of this realme, our merchants and their goods shal
not be subiect to arrest of ancient enemies & doubtfull friends,
as of late yéeres they haue béene.

D   8   F

8 If our nation do not make any conqueſt there, but only vſe trafficke and change of commodities, yet by meane the countrey is not very mightie, but diuided into pety kingdoms, they ſhall not dare to offer vs any great annoy, but ſuch as we may eaſily reuenge with ſufficient chaſtiſement to the vnarmed people there.

9 Whatſoeuer commodities we receiue by the Steelyard merchants, or by our owne merchants from Eaſtland, be it Flaxe, Hempe, Pitch, Tarre, Maſts, Clap-boord, Wainſcot, or ſuch like; the like good may we receiue from the North and Northeaſt part of that countrey neere vnto Cape Briton, in returne for our courſe Woollen clothes, Flanels and Rugges fit for thoſe colder regions.

10 The paſſage to and fro, is thorow the maine Ocean ſea, ſo as we are not in danger of any enemies coaſt.

11 In the voyage, we are not to croſſe the burnt Zone, nor to paſſe thorow frozen ſeas encombred with ice and fogs, but in temperate climate at all times of the yeere: and it requireth not, as the Eaſt Indie voiage doth, the taking in of water in diuers places, by reaſon that it is to be ſailed in fiue or ſix weeks: and by the ſhortneſſe, the merchant may yeerely make two returnes (a factory once being erected there) a matter in trade of great moment.

12 In this trade by the way in our paſſe to and fro, we haue in tempeſts and other haps, all the ports of Ireland to our aid, and no neere coaſt of any enemy.

13 By this ordinary trade we may annoy the enemies to Ireland, and ſuccour the Queenes Maieſties friends there, and in time we may from Virginia yeeld them whatſoeuer commoditie they now receiue from the Spaniard; and ſo the Spaniards ſhall want the ordinary victual that heertofore they receiued yeerely from thence, and ſo they ſhall not continue trade, nor fall ſo aptly in practiſe againſt this gouernment, as now by their trade thither they may.

14 We ſhall, as it is thought, enioy in this voyage, either ſome ſmall Iſlands to ſettle on, or ſome one place or other on the firme land to fortifie for the ſaftie of our ſhips, our men, and our goods, the like whereof we haue not in any forren place of our trafficke, in which reſpect we may be in degree of

more

moze safetie, and moze quiet.

15 The great plentie of Buffe hides, and of many other sundzy kinds of hides there now pzesently to be had, the trade of Whale and Seale fishing, and of diuers other fishings in the great riuers, great bayes, and seas there, shall pzesently defray the charge in good part oz in all of the first enterpzise, and so we shall be in better case than our men were in Russia, where many yeeres were spent, and great summes of money consumed, befoze gaine was found.

16 The great bzoad riuers of that maine that we are to enter into so many leagues nauigable oz poztable into the maine land, lying so long a tract with so excellent and so fertile a soile on both sides, doe seeme to pzomise all things that the life of man doth require, and whatsoeuer men may wish, that are to plant vpon the same, oz to trafficke in the same.

17 And whatsoeuer notable commoditie the soile within oz without doth yeeld in so long a tract that is to be carried out from thence to England, the same riuers so great and deepe, do yeeld no small benefit foz the sure, safe, easie and cheape cariage of the same to shipboozd, be it of great bulke oz of great weight.

18 And in like sozt whatsoeuer commoditie of England the Inland people there shall need, the same riuers doe wozke the like effect in benefit foz the incariage of the same, aptly, easily, and cheaply.

19 If we finde the countrey populous, and desirous to expel vs, and iniuriously to offend vs, that seeke but iust and lawfull trafficke, then by reason that we are lozds of nauigation, and they not so, we are the better able to defend our selues by reason of those great riuers, & to annoy them in many places.

20 Where there be many petie kings oz lozds planted on the riuers sides, and by all likelihood mainteine the frontiers of their seuerall territozies by warres, we may by the aide of this riuer ioine with this king heere, oz with that king there, at our pleasure, and may so with a few men be reuenged of any wzong offered by any of them; oz may, if we will pzoceed with extremitie, conquer, foztifie, and plant in soiles most sweet, most pleasant, most strong, and most fertile, and in the end bzing them all in subiection and to ciuilitie.

21 The knowen abundance of Fresh fish in the riuers, and

D 2   the

the knowen plentie of Fiſh on the ſea coaſt there, may aſſure vs of ſufficient victuall in ſpight of the people, if we will vſe ſalt and induſtrie.

22 The knowen plentie and varietie of Fleſh, of diuers kinds of beaſts at land there, may ſæme to ſay to vs, that we may cheaply victuall our nauies to England for our returnes, which benefit euery where is not found of merchants.

23 The practiſe of the people of the Eaſt Indies, when the Portugals came thither firſt, was to cut from the Portugals their lading of Spice: and hæreby they thought to ouerthrow their purpoſed trade. If theſe people ſhall practiſe the like, by not ſuffering vs to haue any commoditie of theirs without conqueſt, (which requireth ſome time) yet may we mainteine our firſt voyage thither, till our purpoſe come to effect, by the ſea-fiſhing on the coaſts there, and by dragging for pearles, which are ſaid to be on thoſe parts; and by returne of thoſe commodities, the charges in part ſhall be defraied: which is a matter of conſideration in enterpriſes of charge.

24 If this realme ſhall abound to to much with youth, in the mines there of Golde, (as that of Chiſca and Saguenay) of Siluer, Copper, Yron, &c. may be an imployment to the be-nefit of this realme; in tilling of the rich ſoile there for graine, and in planting of Vines there for Wine; or dreſſing of thoſe Vines which grow there naturally in great abundance, O-liues for Oile; Orenge trees, Limons, Figs and Almonds for fruit; Wad, Saffron, and Madder for Diers; Hoppes for Brewers; Hempe, Flaxe; and in many ſuch other things, by imploiment of the ſoile, our people void of ſufficient trades, may be honeſtly imploied, that els may become hurtfull at home.

25 The nauigating of the ſeas in the voyage, and of the great riuers there, will bræd many Mariners for ſeruice, and mainteine much nauigation.

26 The number of raw Hides there of diuers kindes of beaſts, if we ſhall poſſeſſe ſome Iſland there, or ſettle on the firme, may preſently imploy many of our idle people in diuers ſeuerall dreſſings of the ſame, and ſo we may returne them to the people that can not dreſſe them ſo well; or into this realm, where the ſame are good merchandize; or to Flanders, &c. which

preſent

pҙefent gaine at the firſt, raiſeth great incouragement pҙeſent-ly to the enterpҙiſe.

27 Since great waſte Wꝏds be there, of Oake, Cedar, Pine, Wall-nuts, and ſundҙy other ſoҙts, many of our waſte people may be imployed in making of Ships, Hoies, Buſſes and Boats; and in making of Roҗen, Pitch and Tarre, the trꝰs naturall foҗ the ſame, being certeinly knowen to be nꝏre Cape Briton and the Bay of Menan, and in many other places there about.

28 If mines of white oҗ gray marble, Jet, oҗ other rich ſtone be found there, our idle people may be imployed in the mines of the ſame, and in pҗeparing the ſame to ſhape, and ſo ſhaped, they may be caried into this realm as gꝏd balaſt foҗ our ſhips, and after ſerue foҗ noble buildings.

29 Sugar-canes may be planted aſwell as they are now in the South of Spaine, and beſides the imploiment of our idle peop!e, we may receiue the commodity cheaper, and not inrich inſidels oҗ our doubtful friends, of whom now we receiue that commoditie.

30 The daily great increaſe of Wꝏlles in Spaine, and the like in the Weſt Indies, and the great imploiment of the ſame into Cloth in both places, may mꝏue vs to endeuour, foҗ vent of our Cloth, new diſcoueries of peopled regions, where hope of ſale may ariſe; otherwiſe in ſhoҗt time many inconuenien-ces may poſſibly enſue.

31 This land that we purpoſe to direct our courſe to, ly-ing in part in the 40 degrꝳ of latitude, being in like heat as Lisbone in Portugall doth, and in the moҗe Southerly part as the moſt Southerly coaſt of Spaine doth, may by our diligence yꝰld vnto vs beſides Wines and Oiles and Sugars, Oҗen-ges, Limons, Figs, Reſings, Almonds, Pomegranates, Rice, Raw-ſilks ſuch as come from Granada, and diuers commodi-ties foҗ Diers, as Anile and Cochenillio, and ſundҗy other co-lours and materials. Moҗeouer, we ſhall not onely receiue many pҗecious commodities beſides from thence, but alſo ſhal in time finde ample vent of the labour of our pꝏҗe people at home, by ſale of Hats, Bonets, Kniues, Fiſh-hꝏks, Copper kettles, Beads, Lꝏking-glaſſes, Bugles, & a thouſand kinds of other wҗought wares, that in ſhoҗt time may be bҗought in

vſe

vſe among the people of that countrey, to the great reliefe of
the multitude of our poze people, and to the wonderfull en﹣
riching of this realme. And in time, ſuch league & entercourſe
may ariſe betwæene our Stapling ſeats there, and other pozts
of our Northern America, and of the Iſlands of the ſame, that
incredible things, and by few as yet dzeamed of, may ſpædily
follow, tending to the impeachment of our mightie enemies,
and to the common good of this noble gouernment.

The ends of ⎰ 1. To plant Chriſtian religion. ⎱ Oz, to doe all
this voyage ⎱ 2. To trafficke.   ⎰ thzǽ.
are theſe : 3. To conquer.

TO plant Chziſtian religion without conqueſt, will bǽ
hard. Trafficke eaſily followeth conqueſt : conqueſt is
not eaſie. Trafficke without conqueſt ſæmeth poſſible, and
not vneaſie. What is to be done, is the queſtion.

If the people be content to liue naked, and to content them﹣
ſelues with few things of mǽre neceſſity, then trafficke is not.
So then in vaine ſæmeth our voyage, vnleſſe this nature may
be altered, as by conqueſt and other good meanes it may be,
but not on a ſudden. The like whereof appeared in the Eaſt
Indies, vpon the Poztugals ſeating there.

If the people in the Inland be clothed, and deſire to liue in
the abundance of all ſuch things as Europe doth, and haue at
home all the ſame in plentie, yet we can not haue trafficke
with them, by meane they want not any thing that we can
yǽld them.

Admit that they haue deſire to your commodities, and as
yet haue neither Golde, Siluer, Copper, Iron, noz ſufficient
quantitie of other pzeſent commoditie to mainteine the yǽrely
trade : What is then to be done?

Meanes to
bzeed a ſpeꞓ-
dle trade.

The ſoile and climate firſt is to be conſidered, and you are
with Argus eies to ſæ what commoditie by induſtrie of man
you are able to make it to yǽld, that England doth want oz
doth deſire : as foz the purpoſe, if you can make it to yǽld good
Wine, oz good Oile, as it is like you may by the climat, (where
wilde Wines of ſundzy ſozts doe naturally grow already in
great abundance) then your trade may be mainteined. But
admit

admit the soile were in our disposition (as yet it is not) in what time may this be brought about?

For Wine this is to be affirmed, that first the soile lying in 36 or 37 degrées in the temperature of South Spaine, in setting your Vine-plants this yéere, you may haue Wine within thrée yéeres. And it may be that the wilde Vines growing there already, by orderly pruning and dressing at your first arriuall, may come to profit in shorter time.

And planting your Oliue trées this yéere, you may haue Oile within thrée yéeres.

And if the sea shores be flat, and fit for receipt of salt water, and for Salt making, without any annoy of néere freshes, then the trade of Salt onely may mainteine a yéerely nauigation (as our men now trade to the isle of Maio, and the Hollanders to Terra Firma néere the West end of the isle of Margarita.)

But how the naturall people of the countrey may be made skilfull to plant Vines, and to know the vse, or to set Oliue trées, and to know the making of Oile, and withall to vse both the trades, that is a matter of small consideration: but to conquer a countrey or prouince in climate & soile of Italie, Spaine, or the Ilands from whence we receiue our Wines & Oiles, and to man it, to plant it, and to kéepe it, and to continue the making of Wines and Oiles able to serue England, were a matter of great importance both in respect of the sauing at home of our great treasure now yéerely going away, and in respect of the annoyance thereby growing to our enemies. The like consideration would be had, touching a place for the making of Salt, of temperature like those of France, not too too colde, as the Salts of the Northern regions be; nor too too firy, as those be that be made more Southerly than France. In regard whereof, many circumstances are to be considered; and principally, by what meane the people of those parties may be drawen by all courtesie into loue with our nation; that we become not hatefull vnto them, as the Spaniard is in Italie and in the West Indies, and elswhere, by their maner of vsage: for a gentle course without crueltie and tyrannie best answereth the profession of a Christian, best planteth Christian religion; maketh our seating most void of blood, most profitable in trade

A gentle course best to be held.

D 4   of

of merchandiſe, moſt firme and ſtable, and leaſt ſubiect to re-
moue by practiſe of enemies. But that we may in ſeating
there, not be ſubiect wholly to the malice of enemies, and may
be more able to preſerue our bodies, ſhips, and goods in more
ſafetie, and to be knowen to be more able to ſcourge the people
there, ciuill or ſauage, than willing to offer any violence. And
for the more quiet exerciſe of our manurance of the ſoiles
where we ſhall ſeat, and of our manuall occupations, it is to
be wiſhed that ſome ancient captaines of milde diſpoſition and
great iudgement be ſent thither with men moſt ſkilfull in the
arte of fortification ; and that direction be taken that the
mouthes of great riuers, and the Iſlands in the ſame (as
things of great moment) be taken, manned, and fortified ; and
that hauens be cut out for ſafetie of the Nauie, that we may be
lords of the gates and entries, to goe out and come in at pleaſure, and to lie in ſafetie, and be able to command and to con-
trole all within, and to force all forren nauigation to lie out in
open rode ſubiect to all weathers, to be diſperſed by tempeſts
and flawes, if the force within be not able to giue them the en-
counter abroad.

The Red Muſcadell grape, that biſhop Grindall procured
out of Germanie ; the great White Muſcadell ; the Yel-
low grape : the cuts of theſe were wont yeerely to be ſet at
Fulham ; and after one yeeres rooting to be giuen by the biſhop,
and to be ſold by his gardener. Theſe preſently prouided, and
placed in earth, and many of theſe ſo rooted, with ſtore of cuts
vnrooted beſides, placed in tubbes of earth ſhipped at the next
voyage, to be planted in Virginia, may begin Uineyards, and
bring Wines out of hand.

    2 Prouiſion great of wilde Oliue trees may be made out
of this citie ſo then to be caried, to encreaſe great ſtore of ſtocks
to graffe the beſt Oliue on : and Virginia ſtanding in the ſame
degree that The Shroffe the Oliue place doth in Spaine, we
may win that merchandiſe, graffing the wilde.

    3 Sugar-canes, if you can not procure them from the
Spaniſh Iſlands, yet may you by your Barberie merchants
procure them.

    4 There is an herbe in Perſia, whereof Anile is made,
and

and it is also in Barbarie : to procure that by seed or root, were of importance for a trade of merchandise for our clothing countrey.

5　Dad by the seeds you may haue; for you may haue hundreds of bushels in England, as it is multiplied : and hauing soile and labor in Virginia cheape, and the Dad in great value, lying in small roome, it will be a trade of great gaine to this clothing realme : and the thing can not be destroyed by Saluages. The roots of this you may haue in plenty and number comming in the trade : so this may grow in trade within a yeere ready for the merchant.

6　Figge trees of many good kinds may be had hence in barrell, if now presently they be prouided ; and they in that climat will yeeld noble fruit, and feed your people presently, and will be brought in frailes home as merchandise, or in barrell, as Resings also may be.

7　Sawed boords of Sassafras and Cedar, to be turned into small boxes for ladies and gentlewomen, would become a present trade.

8　To the infinite naturall increase of Hogs, to adde a deuice how the same may be fed by roots, acornes, &c. without spoiling your corne, would be of great effect to feed the multitude continually imployed in labour : and the same cheaply bred and salted, and barrelled there and brought home, will be well solde for a good merchandise ; and the barrels after, will serue for our home Herring-fishing; and so you sell your woods and the labour of your cooper.

9　Receiuing the saluage women and their children of both sexes by courtesie into your protection, and imploying the English women and the others in making of Linnen, you shal raise a woonderfull trade of benefit, both to carie into England and also into the Islands, and into the maine of the West Indies, victuall and labour being so cheape there.

10　The trade of making cables and cordage there, will be of great importance, in respect of a cheape maintenance of the Nauie that shall passe to and fro ; and in respect of such Nauie as may in those parties be vsed for the venting of the commodities of England to be brought thither. And Powldauies, &c. made for sailes of the poore Saluages, yeeld to the Nauie a

C　　　　　　　　　great

great helpe, and a great gaine in the trafficke.

But if ſæking reuenge on euery iniurie of the Saluages we ſæke blœd & raiſe war, our Uines, our Oliues, our Figge trées, our Sugar-canes, our Ozenges and Limons, Cozne, Cattell, &c. will be deſtroyed, and trade of merchandiſe in all things ouerthzowen; and ſo the Engliſh nation there planted and to be planted, ſhalbe rœted out with ſwozd and hunger.

Sorts of men which are to be paſſed in
this voyage.

1 MEn ſkilfull in all Minerall-cauſes.
2 Men ſkilfull in all kinde of dzugges.
3 Fiſhermen, to conſider of the ſea fiſhings there on the coaſts, to be reduced to trade hereafter: and others foz the freſh water fiſhings.
4 Salt-makers, to biew the coaſt, and to make triall how rich the ſea-water there is, to aduiſe foz the trade.
5 Huſbandmen, to biew the ſoile, to reſolue foz tillage in all ſozts.
6 Uineyard-men bzed, to ſæ how the ſoile may ſerue foz the planting of Uines.
7 Men bzed in the Shzoffe in South Spaine, foz diſcerning how Oliue trées may be planted there.
8 Others, foz planting of Ozenge trées, Figge trées, Limon trées, and Almond trées; foz iudging how the ſoile may ſerue foz the ſame.
9 Gardeners, to pzœue the ſeuerall ſoiles of the Iſlands, and of our ſetling places, to ſæ how the ſame may ſerue foz all herbs and rœts foz our bictualling; ſince by rough ſeas ſometimes we may want fiſh, and ſince we may want fleſh to bictuall bs, by the malice of the naturall people there: and gardeners foz planting of our common trées of fruit, as Peares, Apples, Plummes, Peaches, Medlers, Apzicoes, Quinces foz conſerues, &c.
10 Lime-makers, to make lime foz buildings.
11 Maſons, Carpenters, &c. foz buildings there.
12 Bzicke-makers and Tile-makers.
13 Men cunning in the art of foztification, that may chuſe
out

out places ſtrong by nature to be fortified, and that can plot out and direct workemen.

14 Choiſe Spade-men, to french cunningly, and to raiſe bulwarks and rampiers of earth for defence and offence.

15 Spade-makers, that may, out of the Wods there, make spades like thoſe of Deuonſhire, and of other ſorts, and ſhouels from time to time for common vſe.

16 Smithes, to forge the yrons of the ſhouels and ſpades, and to make blacke billes and other weapons, and to mend many things.

17 Men that vſe to breake Aſh trées for pike-ſtaues, to be imploied in the Wods there.

18 Others, that finiſh vp the ſame ſo rough hewo, ſuch as in London are to be had.

19 Cwpers, to make caſke of all ſorts.

20 Forgers of pikes heads and of arrow heads, with for- ges, with Spaniſh yron, and with all maner of twles to be ca- ried with them.

21 Fletchers, to renew arrowes, ſince archerie preuaileth much againſt vnarmed people: and gunpowder may ſwne pe- riſh, by ſetting on fire.

22 Bowyers alſo, to make bowes there for néd.

23 Makers of oares, ſince for ſeruice vpon thoſe riuers it is to great purpoſe, for the boats and barges they are to paſſe and enter with.

24 Shipwrights, to make barges and boats, and bigger veſſels, if néd be, to run along the coaſt, and to pierce the great Bayes and Inlets.

25 Turners, to turne targets of Elme and tough wod, for vſe againſt the darts and arrowes of Saluages.

26 Such alſo as haue knowledge to make targets of horne.

27 Such alſo as can make armor of hides vpon moulds, ſuch as were wont to be made in this realme about an hun- dred yéeres ſince, and were called Scotiſh iacks: ſuch armor is light and defenſiue enough againſt the force of Saluages.

28 Tanners, to tanne hides of Buffes, Oxen, &c. in the Iſles where you ſhall plant.

29 White Tawyers of all other ſkinnes there.

30 Men ſkilfull in burning of Sope aſhes, and in making

of Pitch, and Tarre, and Rozen, to be fetched out of Pruſsia and Poland, which are thence to be had for ſmall wages, being there in maner of ſlaues.

The ſeuerall ſorts of trées, as Pines, Firres, Spruſes, Birch and others, are to be boared with great augers a foot or halfe a yard aboue the ground, as they vſe in Veſely towards Languedock and néere Bayona in Gaſcoigne : and ſo you ſhall eaſily and quickly ſée what Gummes, Rozen, Turpentine, Tarre, or liquor is in them, which will quickly diſtill out cléerely without any filthie mixture, and will ſhew what commoditie may be made of them : their goodneſſe and greatneſſe for maſts is alſo to be conſidered.

31 A ſkilfull painter is alſo to be caried with you, which the Spaniards vſed commonly in all their diſcoueries to bring the deſcriptions of all beaſts, birds, fiſhes, trées, townes, &c.

A briefe

A briefe note of the corne, fowles, fruits and beasts of the Inland of *Florida* on the backeside of *Virginia*, taken out of the 44 chapter of the discouery of the said countrey, begun by *Fernando de Soto* gouernour of *Cuba*, in the yeere of our Lord 1539.

He bread which they eat in all the land of Florida, is of Maiz, which is like to course Millet. And in all the Islands and West Indies from the Antiles forward there is this Maiz.

Likewise in Florida there be many Wallnuts, Plummes, Mulberies, & Grapes. They sowe their Maiz, and gather it, euery man his owne croppe. **Their fruits.** The fruits are common to all men, because they grow abundantly in the fields without planting or dressing. In the mountaines there grow Chestnuts; they are somewhat smaller than the Chestnuts of Spaine, which are called Collarínnas. From Rio Grande toward the West, the Walnuts are differing from the other; for they are softer and round like bullets. And from Rio Grande toward Puerto del Spirito Santo Eastward, for the most part they are harder. And the Trées and Nuts are like in fashion vnto those of Spaine. There is in all the countrey a fruit which groweth vpon an herbe or plant like to the herbe called Dogs-tongue, which the Indians doe sowe. The fruit is like vnto the Peres Rial: it is of a very good rellish, and of a pleasant taste. Another herbe groweth in the **These may be the Tunas.** fields, which beareth a fruit nére the ground like to a Strawberie, very pleasant in taste. The Plummes are of two sorts, red and gray, in fashion and bignesse of Walnuts, and haue thrée or foure stones in them. These are better than any in Spaine, and they make better Prunes of them. The want of

E 3   dressing

dressing is perceiued only in the Grapes : which although they be great, yet they haue a great kernell. All the rest of the fruits are very perfect, and lesse hurtfull than those of Spaine.

The beasts of Florida.

There are in Florida many Beares, Lions, Stags, Roe-bucks, Wild-cats, and Conies.

There be many Wild-hennes as bigge as Peacocks, small Partridges like those of Africa, Cranes, Ducks, Rolas, Black-birds, and Sparrowes. There be certeine Blacke birds bigger than Sparrowes and lesser than Stares.

There be Sore-hauks, Faulcons, Gosse-hauks, and all sowles of pray that are in Spaine.

The Indians are well proportioned. Those of the plaine countreys are taller of stature, and better proportioned than those of the mountaines. Those of the Inland are better furnished with corne and wealth of the countrey, than those of the sea coast. The countrey on the sea coast toward the gulfe of Mexico is barren and poore, and the people more warrelike.

The coast beareth from Puerto del Spirito Santo vnto Apa-lache, and from Apalache to Rio de Palmas almost from East to West ; from Rio de Palmas vnto Noua Hi-spania it runneth from North to South. It is a gentle coast, but it hath many sholds and banks or shelues of sand.

A Noet

A Note of such commodities as are found in
Florida *next adioining vnto the South part of* Virginia, taken out of the description of the said countrey,
written by Mounsieur *Rene Landonniere*,
who inhabited there two Som-
mers and one winter.

He countrey of Florida is flat, and diuided with *The trees of Florida.*
diuers riuers, and therefore moist, and is sandy
towards the sea-shore.

    There groweth in those parts great quanti-
tie of Pyne trees, which haue no kernels in the
apples that they beare.

    Their woods are full of Oakes, Walnut trees, blacke Cher-
rie trees, Mulberie trees, Lentiskes which yeeld Masticke, and
Chestnut trees, which are more wilde than those of France.

    There is great store of Cedars, Cypresses, Baies, Palme
trees, Grapes: There is there a kinde of Medlars, the fruit *Good Grapes*
whereof is better then that of France, and bigger. There are
also Plumme trees, which beare very faire fruit, but such as
is not very good.

    There are Raspesses, and a little bery which we call a-
mong vs Blues, which are very good to eat.

    There grow in that countrey a kinde of Rootes, which they
call in their language Hazes, whereof in necessitie they make
bread.

    There is also the tree called Esquine, (which I take to be
the Sassafras) which is very good against the pocks and other
contagious diseases.

    The Beasts best knowen in this countrey are Stagges, *The Beasts of Florida.*
Roes, Deere, Goates, Leopards, Ownces, Lucernes, diuers
sorts of Wolues, wilde Dogges, Hares, Connies, and a cer-

teine kinde of beaſt that differeth little from the Lion of A-
fricke.

The Fowles of Florida.

The Fowles are Turkie Cocks, Partridges, Perrots, Pigeons, Ringdoues, Turtles, Blacke birds, Crowes, Tarcels, Faulcons, Leonards, Herons, Cranes, Storkes, wilde Geeſe, Mallards, Cormorants, Herneſhawes, white, red, blacke, and gray, and an infinit ſort of all wildfoule.

There is ſuch aboundance of Crocodiles, that oftentimes in ſwimming, men are aſſailed by them: Of ſerpents there are many ſorts.

Gold and Siluer.

There is found among the Sauages good quantitie of Gold and Siluer, which is gotten out of the ſhips that are loſt vpon the coaſt: Neuertheleſſe they ſay, that in the mountains of Apalatcy, there are mines of Copper, which I thinke to be Gold.

Store of dies and colours.

There is alſo in this countrey, great ſtore of Graines and Herbes, whereof might be made excellent good dies and pain-tings of all kinde of colours.

They ſowe their Maiz or Corne twice a yeere, to wit, in March and in Iune: and all in one and the ſame ſoile: The ſaid Maiz from the time that it is ſowed, vnto the time that it is gathered, is but three moneths in the ground. They haue al-ſo faire Pumpions and very good Beanes: They haue cer-

Oile in Florida,

teine kinds of oile, wherewith they vſe to annoint them-ſelues.

A briefe extract of the merchantable commodities found in the *South* part of Virginia, *ann*. 1585.
and 1586. Gathered out of the learned worke of
master *Thomas Herriot* , which was there
remaining the space of ele-
uen moneths.

Ilke of Graſe, oꝛ Graſſe-ſilke, the like whereof groweth in Perſia, whereof J haue ſeene
good Grograine made
Woꝛme-ſilke.
Flaxe and Hempe.
Allom.
Wapeih a kinde of earth ſo called by the naturall inhabi-
tants, very like to Terra Sigillata, and by ſome of our Phyſiti-
ons found moꝛe effectuall.
Pitch, Tarre, Roʒen, and Turpentine: there are thoſe
kinds of trees that yeld them aboundantly and in great ſtoꝛe.
Saſſafras, called by the inhabitants Wynauk: of whoſe
ſoueraigne and manifold vertues, reade Monardes the Phiſi-
cian of Sinile, in his booke entituled in Engliſh: The ioyfull
newes from the Weſt Indies.
Cedar.
Vines of two ſoꝛts.
Oile: there are two ſoꝛts of Wall-nuts, both holding oile.
Furthermoꝛe, there are three ſeuerall kindes of Berries, in
the foꝛme of Oake Acoꝛnes, which alſo by the experience and
vſe of the inhabitants, we finde to yeld very good and ſweete
Oile. There are alſo Beares, which are commonly very fat,
and in ſome places there are many, their fatneſſe becauſe it is
ſo liquid, may well be termed Oyle, and hath many ſpeciall
vſes.

F   Furres.

Furres.

Ottars, Marternes, and Lucernes.

Deere skinnes.

Ciuet Cattes.

Iron.

Copper. The foresaid Copper, we also found by triall to hold Siluer.

Pearle. One of our company, a man of skill in such matters, had gathered together from the Sauages, aboue fiue thousand.

Sweet Gummes of diuers kinds, and many other Apothecary drugs.

Dies of diuers kinds.

There is Shoemake, well knowen and vsed in England for blacke; the seed of an herbe called Wasebur, little small rootes called Chappacor, and the barke of a tree called by the inhabitants, Tangomockonomindge, which Dies are for diuers sorts of red.

Commodities in *Virgina*, knowen to yeeld victuals.

PAgatowr or Mays, which is their principall corne.

Okindgier, called by vs Beanes.

Wickonzour, called by vs Pease.

Macocquer, called by vs, Pompions, Mellons, & Gourds.

An herbe which in Dutch is called Melden, being a kinde of Orage, &c.

An herbe in forme of a Marigold, sixe foot in height, taken to be Planta Solis.

Vppowoc, or Tabacco, of great estimation among the Sauages.

Rootes.

OPenauck, a kinde of Rootes of round forme, as bigge as Wall-nuts, some farre greater. Monardes calleth them Beades, or Pater nostri of Sancta Helena, and master Brereton Ground Nuts.

Okeepenauk, are Rootes of round shape found in dry grounds

groundes, the inhabitants vſe to boile and eat many of them.

Tſinaw, a kinde of Roote much like vnto that which in England is called the China Roote, brought from the Eaſt Indies.

Coſcuſhaw, a Roote taken to be that which the Spaniards in the Weſt Indies, doe call Caſſauy.

Habaſcon, a Roote of hot taſte, almoſt of the forme and bigneſſe of a Parſnep.

Leekes differing little from ours in England.

Fruites.

CHeſtnuts there are in diuers places great ſtore, vſed diuers waies for fod.

Walnuts there are two kinds, and of them infinit ſtore in many places, where are very great woods for many miles together, the third part of the trees are Walnut trees, they vſe them for meate, and make a milke of them of verie pleaſant taſte, and holeſome.

Medlers, a kinde of very good fruit, they are as red as cherries, and very luſhous ſweet.

Mutaqueſunnauk, a kinde of pleaſant fruit, almoſt of the ſhape and bigneſſe of Engliſh Peares, but they are of a perfect red colour, as well within as without, they grow on a plant whoſe leaues are very thicke and full of prickles, as ſharpe as needles: ſome, which haue beene in Noua Hiſpania, where they haue ſeene that kinde of red Die of exceeding great price, which is called Cochenile, to grow, do deſcribe his plant right like vnto this of Mutaqueſunnauk: howbeit the Cochenile is not the fruit, but a graine found on the leaues of the plant, and ſtricken off vpon ſheetes, and dried in the ſunne.

Theſe plants are called Tunas alſo, whereof there be three ſorts: that which beareth no fruit bringeth foorth the Cochenile.

Grapes there are of two ſorts, which I mentioned in the merchantable commodities.

Strawberies there are, as good and as great as in any Engliſh garden.

Mulberies,
Apple-crabbes,　} ſuch as we haue in England.
Hurts, or Hurtleberies,

Sacquenummener a kinde of berries almoſt like vnto Capers but ſomewhat greater, which grow together in cluſters vpon a plant oz hearbe that is found in hollow waters, being boiled eight oz nine houres according to their kinde, are very good meat and holſome, otherwiſe if they be eaten, they will make a man foz the time franticke oz extremely ſicke.

A Reed which beareth a ſeed almoſt like vnto our Rie oz Wheat and being boiled is good meat.

In our trauells in ſome places, we found wilde Peaſe like vnto ours in England, but that they were leſſe, which are alſo good meat.

A kind of Berry like vnto an Acorne, of fiue ſozts, growing on ſeuerall kindes of trées : the one ſozt is called Sagatemener, the ſecond, Oſamener, the third Pummuckoner. the inhabitants vſe to dzy them vpon hurdles like Malt in England. when they vſe them, they firſt water them till they be ſoft, and then being ſod, they make loues of bzead of them. of theſe thzée kindes alſo the inhabitants doe vſe to make ſwéet oile.

The fourth ſozt is called Sapummener, which being boiled oz perched be like vnto roſted Cheſnuts ; of this ſozt they make bzead alſo.

The fift ſozt is called Mangummenauk, the very Acozne of their kind of Oake; being dzied as the reſt, and after watered, they boile them, and their ſeruants, and ſomtimes the chiefe themſelues eate them with their fiſh and fleſh.

Beaſts.

Dⱸere, vp into the countrey very great, and in ſome places, great ſtoze.

Conies, of a gray colour like vnto hares : they make mantles of the furre oz flue of their ſkinnes.

Saquenuckot and Maquowoc, two kindes of ſmall beaſts greater then Conies, which are very good meat.

Squirels, which are of a gray colour, we haue taken and eaten.

Beares, which are of blacke colour. They are good meat. And being hunted they climbe vp into trées and are killed by the Saluages with their arrowes, and ſometimes by vs with our Caliuers.

The Lion is ſometimes killed by the Saluages and eaten.
Wolues

Wolues oz Wolulsh dogges.

I haue the names of eight and twenty sozts of beasts dispersed in the maine, of which their are onely twelue kindes by vs as yet discouered.

Fowle

TVrkie cocks and Turkie hennes, Stock-doues, and Partriges, Cranes, hernes, and in Winter great stoze of Swannes, and Geese.

There are also Parrots, Falcons, and Marlin haukes.

Of all sozts of foules I haue the names in the countrey language of fowzescoze and sire.

Fish.

STurgions, Herrings, Porpoises, Troutes, Rayes, Old-wiues, Mullets, Plaice, and very many other sozts of very excellent fish.

Seacrabs, Oisters, great, small, round, long: Muscles, Scalops, Periwincles, and Creuises.

Seekanauk, a kinde of crustie shell-fish, which is god meate, about a foot in bzedth, hauing a crusty taile, many legges like a Crabbe, and her eyes in her backe. They are found in shallowes of water, and sometimes on the shoze.

Tortoises both of land and sea kinde; they are very god meats and their egges also:

F 3 Certeine

Certaine briefe testimonies touching sundry rich
mines of Gold, Siluer, and Copper, in part found and in
part constantly heard of, in North *Florida*, and the Inland
of the Maine of *Virginia*, and other countreys there vnto
on the North part neere adioining, gathered out of
the works, all (one excepted) extant in print,
of such as were personall trauellers
in those countries

1

I take these
to be the peo-
ple toward
Cibola, clad in
mantels of
cotten.

 N the second relation of Iaques Cartier the 12
chapter he reporteth that he vnderstood by
Donnacona the king of the countrey, and o-
thers, that to the Southwest of Canada there
are people clad with cloth, as the French were,
very honest, and many inhabited townes, and
that they haue great store of Gold and red Copper, &c.

2

In the discouery of the Inland of Florida farre to the North
begun by Fernando de Soto, gouernour of Cuba in the yeere
1539. (and to be seene in print in the hands of Master Richard Hackluyt) The Indians in many places farre distant the
one from the other gaue them often and certaine aduertise-
ment, that beyond the mountaines Northward there were
mines of Gold at a place called by them Chisca, and some
shewed the maner which the Indians vsed in refining the
same. This place in mine opinion cannot be farre from the
great riuer that falleth into the Southwest part of the Bay of
Chesepioc.

3

The Indians enformed Mounsieur Rene Laudonniere in
Florida, that there were mines of red mettall, which they call
in their language Sieroa Pira, in the muuntaines of Apalatcy,
which vpon triall made thereof by the French was found perfect Gold, as appeareth Pagina 352. In the third volume of
the English voiages, and in the same relation there is very often

ten mention of Siluer and excellent perfect and faire perles found by the french in those parts.

In the late discouerie of New Mexico made by Antonio de Espeio on the backe side of Virginia extant in Spanish and English in the third volume of the English voyages paginis 303. &c. there is mention of rich Siluer mines (and sometimes of Gold in aboundance) eleuen or twelue times found as they trauelled Northward, by men very skilfull in minerall matters, which went in the voyage for that purpose. The large description and chart of which voyage containing great numbers of townes and diuers great riuers discouered in that action made in Mexico by Francisco Xamuscado 1585 being intercepted afterward by the English at sea, we haue in London to be shewed to such as shall haue occasion to make vse of the same.

¶ The constant report of many of the Saluages to the worshipfull Master Ralfe Lane then gouernour of the English colonie in Virginia of the rich mine of Wassador or Gold at a place by them named Chaunis Temoatam, twentie daies iourney ouerland from the Mangoaks, set downe by himselfe at large in the first part of his relation of the said countrey of Virginia, extant in the third volume of the English voyages pagina 258. is much to be regarded and considered by those that intend to prosecute this new enterprise of planting nere vnto those parts.

I could giue large information of the rich copper mine in the East side of the Bay of Menan within 30 or 40. leagues to the Southwest of Cape Breton, whereof I my selfe haue seene aboue an hundred pieces of the copper, and haue shewed some part thereof to diuers knightes of qualitie, as also of Salt as good as that of Buruage in France, found nere that Bay, and could make proofe of the testimonie of the Saluages touching a Siluer mine in another Bay within two or three leagues to the west of the aforesaid Bay of Menan : But I reserue a further relation hereof to a more conuenient time and place.

Yf it please any man to read the Summarie of Gonsaluo de Ouiedo extant in part in the English decads, of the voyage of Sebastian Cabote along this coast of Virginia and Norumbega:

.F 4

bega: And the short relation of Iohn de Verarsana, which ranged the said coast long after him in the yeere 1524. which is also to be seene in the third volume of the English voyages pagine 298. he shall finde often mention of rich Minerals and store of excellent copper, which so long agoe they saw among the Saluages, they being the first knowen Christians that euer saw those coasts. So that it were more then wilful madnesse to doubt of rich mines to be in the aforesaid countreys.

*

FINIS.